1001 WAYS TO
SUCCESS

ARCTURUS

ISBN 978-1-4351-4638-9

Manufactured in China

2   4   6   8   10   9   7   5   3

Contents

Introduction

We all dream of succeeding at something, even if each of us has a different idea of what success really means. For some, it is all about status, power, and wealth. For others, it is simply about finding peace, fulfilment and happiness. And then there are others still who do not yet know where their true passion lies; for them success seems like a mythical city absent from their map of life. This little book has been written to try and help everyone who yearns for a better tomorrow, by exploring the many different types of success, and by offering insights into how you might discover, and attain, your own most cherished goals. Successful people from all walks of life share their advice, from the profound to the playful, and from the ancient past to the modern day. Whether you just need a little extra motivation, or a pick-me-up after a setback, this treasury of wisdom will help you as you travel along the road to success. It serves as a constant reminder that, no matter what your own personal dreams of success may be, those dreams are always within your reach.

What is Success?

How do we define success? What things in life are truly worth striving for, and how do we know when we have achieved our ambitions?

Fame and wealth are not the same as success, and sometimes you may have to choose which of them you really want.

No matter what your definition of success is, you cannot succeed without first trying.

You have to go out and find success; it will not come to find you.

Making others happy is a type of success.

You can have anything you want, but not everything you want. Decide what is most important to you and if you achieve that, you have succeeded.

A successful person needs: appreciation, ambition, aspiration, action, accretion, application, attention, audacity, ability, artfulness, achievements, and awakenings.

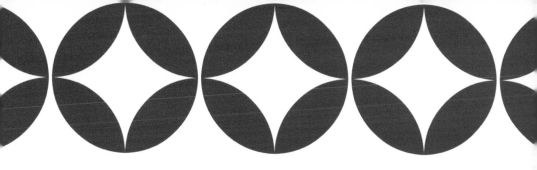

'Overnight success' doesn't really happen overnight: it happens after years of dedication.

You are almost certainly already a success. Go back through your past and look for moments when you achieved something. If you managed it previously, you can manage it again.

If you commit whole-heartedly to your dreams, they are much more likely to come true.

Success is prized because it is difficult. If it was easy then nobody would care about becoming successful.

Exceeding expectations is one of the major steps on the path to success.

A man is a success if he gets up in the morning and goes to bed at night and in between does what he wants to do.
Bob Dylan

Other people may consider you successful or unsuccessful, but it is whether you consider yourself successful that really matters.

Don't just dream of success for yourself – dream of success for others too.

Being successful means being: brave, brilliant, bright, bold, big-hearted, business-like, benevolent, brainy, breathtaking, bubbly, and beautiful.

If you are truly happy then you need not worry about becoming successful. Anyone who is truly happy is already successful.

You will never be successful if you try to please everybody.

17

There are many different types of success, but every single one of them requires hard work.

Success is always temporary – so make sure whatever you are trying to succeed in is fun.

Getting lucky is not the same as becoming successful. You won't feel truly fulfilled unless you feel a genuine sense of achievement.

Success is 1% inspiration and 99% perspiration.

Cultivate being: committed, courageous, cunning, constant, capable, clever, contented, calculating, calm, candid, caring, certain, charismatic, cheerful, classy, cogent, competitive, confident, cool, creative, curious, convivial, and conscientious.

Failure comes when you quit. If you are trying then you are succeeding.

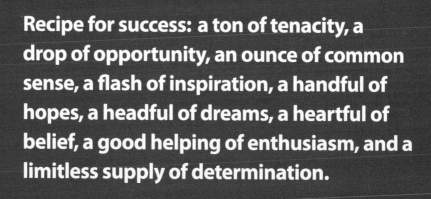

Recipe for success: a ton of tenacity, a drop of opportunity, an ounce of common sense, a flash of inspiration, a handful of hopes, a headful of dreams, a heartful of belief, a good helping of enthusiasm, and a limitless supply of determination.

Find an opportunity and you are half way to finding success.

Success begins when you believe that something is possible.

What appears to be a failure is often just a stepping-stone to success.

Success is not about being wealthy: many wealthy people would readily admit to being failures in other aspects of their life.

The successful self has: self-control, self-belief, self-discipline, self-knowledge, and self-confidence.

In terms of finding success, the safe option is usually the wrong option.

Don't quit – and do be: decisive, daring, defiant, direct, driven, dashing, determined, diligent, delightful, different, dependable, discriminating, dazzling, and dynamic.

There is no such thing as an individual success: we all need a little help, somewhere along the way.

You can't become successful by pretending to be someone you are not.

Success consists of going from failure to failure without loss of enthusiasm. *Winston Churchill*

However far away success appears to be, it is always in your own hands.

Success cannot happen without change, so embrace all changes – even those changes that seem frightening at first.

As many people have been destroyed by success as have been destroyed by failure, so make sure you know what you really want before you go looking for it.

You need the right attitude in order to succeed. Enthusiasm is as important as ability.

Being part of somebody else's success is as sweet as succeeding yourself.

Expect success if you are: enthusiastic, eager, excellent, excited, earnest, entertaining, ebullient, effective, eloquent, extraordinary, encouraging, engaging, energetic, and effusive.

Putting yourself in someone else's shoes often helps you take an important step forward on the road to success.

Don't take foolish risks, but don't be foolish enough to never take risks.

Make sure you can recognize success: sometimes it comes so gradually that you do not even notice it.

Eighty per cent of success is showing up. *Woody Allen*

There is very little difference between success and progress.

To be truly considered successful you need to share your success with others.

Success doesn't always bring happiness, but happiness is always a form of success.

You become successful by doing, not dreaming.

There is no such thing as a 'modest success'. Every success is a big success.

Success is not measured by what you take from the world, but by what you give to the world.

For success find: flexibility, fearlessness, fortitude, familiarity, frankness, flair, friendship, flamboyance, firmness, focus, and faith.

He has achieved success who has lived well, laughed often and loved much; who has gained the respect of intelligent men and the love of little children; who has filled his niche and accomplished his task; who has left the world better than he found it, whether by an improved poppy, a perfect poem, or a rescued soul; who has never lacked appreciation of earth's beauty or failed to express it; who has always looked for the best in others and given them the best he had; whose life was an inspiration; whose memory a benediction. *Bessie Stanley*

When opportunity knocks at your door, invite her in. She is a close friend of success.

The heart, the mind, and the soul must all be successful together, otherwise it is not true success.

A small success should be welcomed as warmly as a large one, for success often snowballs.

Success is making the right choice when faced with many alternatives.

Judge your success not by where you have got to, but where you have come from and what you have overcome in order to succeed.

Being good at what you do is not what leads to success. Being the very best you can be leads to success.

If you always do what you've always done, then you'll always get what you've always had. Success comes from looking honestly at yourself and learning from your mistakes.

Success is having a positive impact upon the world. The greater the impact, the greater the success.

My definition of success is control.

Kenneth Branagh

What was successful for you yesterday may not be successful for you tomorrow: be willing to adapt.

Check your goals regularly, as there is no point achieving them if they are wrong.

Great successes are generally: giving, grafters, go-getters, generous, grateful, gifted, genuine, gracious, good-natured, and gritty.

There is nothing complicated about success: it is simply living life exactly the way you want to live it.

To follow without halt, one aim; there is the secret of success. And success? What is it? I do not find it in the applause of the theatre; it lies rather in the satisfaction of accomplishment. *Anna Pavlova*

You can be successful as many times as you like – just remember to enjoy each and every success.

Count the number of people whose lives you have improved. The higher the number, the more successful you can consider yourself to be.

Success is a habit: small, regular successes lead to larger ones.

To burn always with this hard, gem-like flame, to maintain this ecstasy, is success in life.
Walter Pater

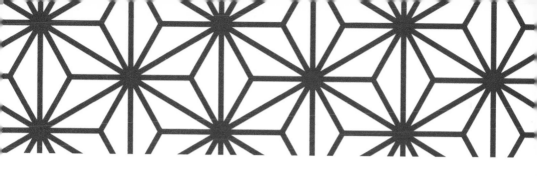

Invite success by improving your: intelligence, imagination, independence, ideas, influence, intensity, insatiability, and inspiration.

Success is doing what you value, and doing it well.

Success is contagious: you can catch it by surrounding yourself with positive people.

A true success story never ends.

My definition of success is to live your life in a way that causes you to feel a ton of pleasure and very little pain – and because of your lifestyle, have the people around you feel a lot more pleasure than they do pain.
Tony Robbins

You cannot measure your success, because it lies within the lives of those you have helped.

Whichever path you take to success, be sure to enjoy every step of the way.

45

Pursuing success half-heartedly will always lead to failure.

If you can enjoy what life offers rather than complaining about what life doesn't offer, you are well on the way to success.

Success is always relative, never absolute.

To me success means effectiveness in the world, that I am able to carry my ideas and values into the world – that I am able to change it in positive ways.

Maxine Hong Kingston

Just be: jovial, jubilant, joyful, jolly, and judicious. Never jealous!

Success is often closest when it looks furthest away.

By trying your hardest you make it easy for success to appear.

A good plan violently executed right now is far better than a perfect plan executed next week.
General George Patton

You will never succeed if you listen to those who claim that what you are trying to do is impossible.

The right time to start trying to be successful is always *right now*.

The sweet smell of success comes from the flowering of a dream.

I must admit that I personally measure success in terms of the contributions an individual makes to her or his fellow human beings. *Margaret Mead*

Putting your heart and soul into everything you do is a type of success in itself.

Do things you love doing, and you will find success surprises you when you least expect it.

Success does not discriminate: no matter who you are, or where you have come from, you too can be successful.

Keep being: keen, kinetic, kissable, kaleidoscopic, knockout, knowledgeable, and kind.

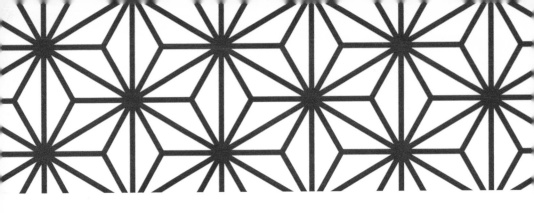

You cannot buy success; you have to work for it.

Success is a destination with thousands of different roads leading to it. It doesn't matter which you take as long as you get there in the end.

A big shot is just a little shot who kept on shooting.

Look at the success of others and ask yourself these two questions: Why not me? Why not now?

True success comes when you try something you think is difficult: if it seems easy then you will not feel successful even if you accomplish it.

It's simply a matter of doing what you do best and not worrying about what the other fellow is going to do.
John R. Amos

Success lies in understanding the difference between what you can and cannot do, and choosing to do the things you can do, well.

Making it means: modesty, mindfulness, moving mountains, managing, majesty, mercy, meticulousness, and marketability.

Thoughts are all very well, but it is only when you turn them into actions that you can consider yourself successful.

Nobody ever found success without taking chances.

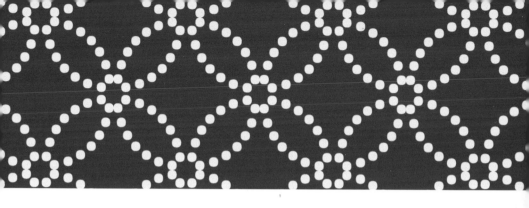

If you find it in your heart to care for somebody else, you will have succeeded. Maya Angelou.

The 'u' in success is you: always strive to be the best you can.

It is not titles that honour men, but men that honour titles. *Spinoza*

Use the bricks others throw at you to build a bridge to success.

The road to success is always under construction.

'Success is just a matter of luck': so say those who have failed.

If in doubt say 'yes' rather than 'no', say 'I will' rather than 'I might', and say 'today' rather than 'tomorrow'.

Success comes from knowing that you did your best to become the best that you are capable of becoming. *John Wooden*

Where you are right now doesn't matter, as long as you are moving in the right direction.

Nail your dreams by: nurturing, navigation, neutrality, niceness, nonchalance, nobility, novelty, and naturalness.

In the end, success is whatever you decide it is. Nobody else's definition of it matters nearly as much as your own.

Finding the Way

Don't dream it, be it: a look at the many different steps we can take towards attaining our most cherished goals.

The first step to achieving something is to believe that you can achieve it.

**Don't try to be *something* –
try to be *someone*.**

Even experts can be wrong sometimes. Take advice, but if you have your heart set on something then don't take no for an answer.

If you stay in the game for long enough, sooner or later you will be in the right place at the right time.

To travel hopefully is a better thing than to arrive, and the true success is to labour.
Robert Louis Stevenson

Persevere, but don't be a fool: if something clearly isn't working then it is time to try something else.

You are more likely to win victory if you pick your battles carefully.

Biting off more than you can chew is better than starving yourself of challenges.

Diligence is the mother of good luck.

Benjamin Franklin

No matter how successful you already are, you can always improve yourself a little further.

The most satisfying success of all is the success that others told you was impossible.

Paper fires produce more light than heat. Build your success on firm foundations so that it can survive the occasional storm.

Use the past as your springboard, not as an excuse.

If fortune smiles on you, pass that smile on to others.

What is the point of chasing success if you never have the time to enjoy it? Make sure you relax and bask in your success now and then.

People are beginning to see that the first requisite to success in life is to be a good animal. *Herbert Spencer*

Obviously, try to be: observant, outstanding, omniscient, opinionated, opportunistic, out-going, outspoken, overactive – and always okay.

Don't let success go to your head: if you don't keep your feet on the ground you can easily lose everything that you worked so hard to achieve.

If you find your success feels somewhat hollow, then reassess your goals and begin again. The problem does not lie with success, but rather with what you have chosen to succeed at.

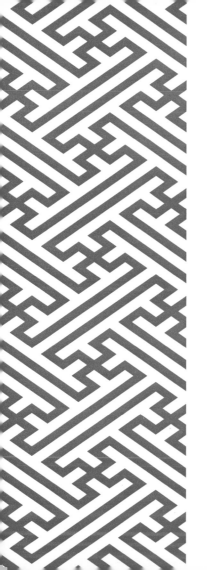

Your character determines whether or not you are successful. Character is more important than ability or intelligence.

Better is the enemy of good.

Steady blows break the rock.

Welsh proverb

Don't blame setbacks on bad luck. Look for the reasons why you failed. If you blame your defeats on bad luck then it follows that your victories are only due to good luck. The successful person learns to take responsibility for their lives.

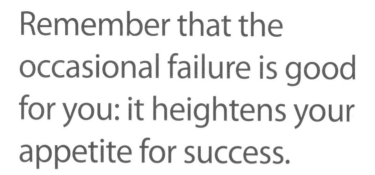

Remember that the occasional failure is good for you: it heightens your appetite for success.

Be kind to yourself, otherwise you will build obstacles to your own success.

To win the war you may have to lose the occasional battle.

Think of your perfect epitaph. That will tell you what is most important to you in life.

Always have a plan B.

Listen to your heart rather than the disparaging remarks of others.

The toughest thing about being a success is that you've got to keep on being a success.
Irving Berlin

Lots of people have good ideas – it is learning how to turn those ideas into actions that leads to success.

Make every moment count. Wasting time will thwart your dreams of success.

Several studies have shown that performance improves when workers are offered incentives in return for increased productivity. Give yourself a 'bonus' if you manage to hit a challenging target: a little bit of self-indulgence will motivate you to succeed.

Most of the successful people I've known are the ones who do more listening than talking. *Bernard Baruch*

Doing a little, and doing it well, is better than trying to do a great deal and doing it badly.

Perfect your: persistence, passion, preparation, planning, perseverance, personality, popularity, playfulness, practicality, proficiency, pride, punctuality, patience, and productivity.

Everyone has their own place in the world. If you find where you best fit, you are more likely to succeed.

If you constantly build yourself up, nobody can tear you down.

The bigger they come the harder they fall.

Bob Fitzsimmons

It is hard to succeed entirely on your own: cultivate networks and don't be too proud to ask for help sometimes.

Only the deluded think they know everything. Embracing the fact that you have much to learn can help you to succeed.

Failures tend to believe in luck – the successful believe in cause and effect.

If you don't know where you are going, you will end up somewhere you never wanted to be.

Beware of those who promise easy success in return for a fee. If you don't stand for something then you'll fall for anything.

Success can lead to complacency – and complacency can lead to failure. Be proud of your successes, but make sure they spur you on to greater things.

If you try to do nothing you will always succeed.

You can believe you can, or you can believe you can't. Either way you are probably right.

You can't climb the ladder of success with your hands in your pockets.

To whom much is given, much is required.
John F. Kennedy

Revel in your: realism, resolution, respectability, rejuvenation, risk-taking, reasoning, radicalism, rarity, rationality, ruthlessness, rebelliousness, receptivity, relevance, remarkableness, responsibility, rigour, romanticism, resourcefulness, and resilience.

The fastest time for the marathon in the 1896 Olympic Games was less than a minute faster than the required entry time for many modern marathons. The improvement is not the result of people today being physically faster, but the result of better training and higher levels of dedication. Practice, and work hard, and you will succeed.

Simplify whenever you can. Over-complicating makes everything seem harder to achieve.

To be afraid of failure is to fail before you have even started.

If you take your eye off the ball you will end up with a black eye and a lost ball.

To succeed you must add to the vast rich tapestry of humanity. It does not matter if you are only a single thread, but aim to be a thread of pure gold.

Even Superman has to go back to being Clark Kent sometimes.

If your heart is not really in something then you will never succeed at it.

Nobody expects you to be perfect, but by fixing things when they go wrong, and learning from the experience, you can become ever better at what you do.

Be humble: the world is not all about you.

Be prepared for the fact that you will have to overcome many obstacles, and that when you do, others may not be interested in the journey you took. They will see only that you became successful, so you must congratulate yourself on the hard work it took to make success happen.

Before you dig for victory, make sure the soil is fertile.

For every one of us that succeeds, it's because there's somebody there to show you the way out. The light doesn't always necessarily have to be in your family; for me it was teachers and school. *Oprah Winfrey*

Successful people show: sacrifice, strength, skill, satisfaction, subtlety, stylishness, sophistication, seductiveness, singularity, sincerity, and spontaneity.

If you can grab an opportunity then it will lead you to many more opportunities.

Make success your friend, not your god.

Love your work rather than the success it may or may not bring you.

Difficult can be transformed into Easy with the right mindset.

A loving person is admired more than a successful person: don't sacrifice love for success.

Smell the rose rather than complaining that it has thorns.

Change, and change again. If you are not constantly changing then you are not succeeding.

When you have difficult choices to make, tell yourself that you already know what to do. It's just a matter of waiting until your heart speaks to you.

When the effective leader is finished with his work, the people say it happened naturally. *Lao Tse*

You cannot know how long the journey ahead of you is. But it cannot begin without one small first step.

You cannot succeed if you are not ruthlessly honest with yourself.

Never climb over others in your desperation to reach for the stars.

The quality of what you do is more important than the quantity.

Good things come to those who try, and try again.

Try and distinguish between what you want and what you really need. If you focus on what you need then you are more likely to succeed.

When nothing seems to help, I go and look at a stonecutter hammering away at his rock perhaps a hundred times without as much as a crack showing in it. Yet at the hundred and first blow it will split in two, and I know it was not that blow that did it, but all that had gone before. *Jacob August Riis*

It is easy to kid yourself that you've done your best, but you can't kid your way to success.

Encouraging others often results in you encouraging yourself too.

Not doing more than the average is what keeps the average down. *William M Winans*

To achieve success try: truthfulness, tolerance, thoughtfulness, trust, targeting, timing, tactfulness, talent, thankfulness, tranquillity, transparency, taste, and training.

Be like the tree that bends in the wind but has its roots deep in the ground.

If you fall down seven times, then get up eight times.

All that's really worth doing is what we do for others.

Spend less than you earn. Having a 'rainy day' fund will help you when times get really tough.

Help others get what they want and you may well find that you get what you want too.

Write a list of successful people you respect, be they friends, neighbours or celebrities. Learn from their example and listen to their advice.

Smile! People are more willing to open up when they see a friendly face.

Be excellent at what you do, and be patient enough to keep doing it, and success will surely follow.

There's no such thing as an 'ill wind' if you know how to set your sails correctly.

Be quick to give compliments: others are more likely to help you if they feel their efforts are appreciated.

Friendly competition with others can spur you to greater heights, but don't engage in petty feuds.

I know the price of success: dedication, hard work, and an unremitting devotion to the things you want to see happen.
Frank Lloyd Wright

Remember that life is short, and in the grand scheme of things any success you achieve will be fleeting. Treasure every moment.

A successful person knows that you dance differently depending on the music being played.

Give your best to others, and others will give you their best in return.

Try and surprise yourself with what you can achieve.

Have high standards, but ensure those standards are realistic too.

Being responsible for yourself is a full time job: don't moonlight as a judge of others.

Learn to control your temper: getting angry with life only makes problems seem more difficult to solve.

Life is not a rehearsal. Make sure your dreams are centre stage.

Good leaders must first become good servants.
Robert Greenleaf

Imagine yourself as a success. If you can feel, touch, and taste success in your mind then you are halfway to experiencing it for real.

Contribute as much as you can, whenever you can.

Make an effort to learn and remember the names of those you meet. If you show that others matter to you, you'll find that your path to success will become a lot easier.

Understand yourself, and be: undeniable, unbiased, unbelievable, uplifting, unassuming, unusual, ultra-determined, unerring, unexpected, unflappable, unpredictable, understanding, unswerving, unyielding, useful, and upbeat.

No matter how busy you are, always remember that nothing is ever lost by courtesy.

Jump out of bed in the morning. As soon as you wake up, adopt a positive and enthusiastic attitude. Strive to maintain that attitude throughout the day.

Trust in yourself. If you don't, then how will others trust you?

Do what you say you are going to do, when you say you are going to do it.

Set daily goals for yourself, and remind yourself of what they are every couple of hours. It is all too easy to get sidetracked and lose focus.

Get out of your comfort zone. It doesn't matter what you choose to do, but push yourself to try something unfamiliar now and then. Taking risks is necessary in order to achieve success.

Keep a diary. Make note of what happened during each day, and whether what happened moved you closer to success or further away.

Study successful people: you can't win unless you understand the rules of the game.

Dream, but don't daydream. Set aside time for relaxation, but don't allow yourself to bunk off when you are meant to be working.

Everybody feels self-doubt from time to time. Courage is about overcoming fear, not pretending you don't feel afraid.

Who dares wins.

Motto of the Special Air Service

Attract an opposite – if you can find a friend or partner who has skills and talents that you lack, then both of you can benefit from teaming up together.

Starting from scratch is not the same as throwing in the towel. Never quit, but be prepared to take a radically different approach if you find your current approach isn't working.

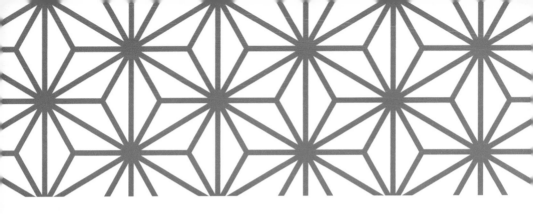

Channel your passion – you need to shine your light like a laser rather than like a floodlight.

Don't become so absorbed with success that you cease to be a good friend. Friends are allies that can speed you on your way to success.

The will to conquer is the first condition of victory. *Marshal Foch*

If what you are striving for doesn't feel as though it requires much courage, then you are probably doing something wrong.

Nothing is more precious than life: don't give control of yours to other people.

Everything passes, and sooner rather than later. Treasure the good times and when times are bad remind yourself that this, too, shall pass.

Success is more permanent when you achieve it without destroying your principles. *Walter Cronkite*

The formula for success is hope plus determination.

Win success with: willingness, warmth, wishes, wisdom, wholeheartedness, wonder, wanting, watchfulness, wit, worth, wild ways, wholeness – and work, work, work!

The Heart of Success

Success is never achieved entirely by, or for, an individual. How do we form successful relationships with others, be they partners, friends, family, or those we are meeting for the very first time?

The art of love is largely the art of persistence. *Albert Ellis*

A successful partnership halves your fears and doubles your joy.

Become the kind of person that you would like to be with.

Success is not worth having unless you have loved ones to share it with.

It is often easier to forgive an enemy than a loved one, but you must learn to do both in order to form successful relationships.

My wife has been my closest friend, my closest advisor. And … she's not somebody who looks to the limelight, or even is wild about me being in politics. And that's a good reality check on me. When I go home, she wants me to be a good father and a good husband. And everything else is secondary to that. *Barack Obama*

There are a million different ways to tell someone you love them – find a new one every day.

Passion fades, but respect, trust, and friendship endure.

The twin pillars of a strong family are love and compromise.

Heartbreak is nature's way of saving you from the wrong partner.

What counts in making a happy marriage is not so much how compatible you are, but how you deal with incompatibility.
George Levinger

True love is about accepting another person as they are, rather than trying to change them into the person we would ideally like them to be.

When you fish for love, bait with your heart, not your brain. *Mark Twain*

The more tightly you cling to past heartbreaks the less able you are to embrace future loves.

Learn to love the differences between yourself and others, as well as the things you have in common.

Children learn everything important the same way: by example.

The quickest way to get somebody interested in you is to show them that you are truly interested in them.

To nourish children and raise them against odds is in any time, any place, more valuable than to fix bolts in cars or design nuclear weapons.
Marilyn French

It is not always wisdom that comes from the mouths of babes – but it is very often the truth!

Love is never a one-way street – learning to give is vital for a successful relationship.

The weak harbour grudges – the strong forgive.

No road is too long with good company.

Mistaking lust for love is the most common cause of relationship break-ups.

Families have always shown remarkable resiliency… their strengths resemble the elasticity of a spider web, a gull's skillful flow with the wind, the regenerating power of perennial grasses, the cooperation of an ant colony, and the persistence of a stream carving canyon rocks. These are not the strengths of fixed monuments but living organisms. This resilience is not measured by wealth, muscle, or efficiency but by creativity, unity, and hope. *Ben Silliman*

The happiest families are those who share their happiness with other families.

Your friends are those you like to be with; your loved ones are those you cannot imagine being without.

Success in marriage does not come merely through finding the right mate, but through being the right mate. *Barnett R. Brickner*

Don't rush to fill silences – not all of them are uncomfortable. Sometimes sharing silence together is as rewarding as sharing a conversation.

Don't give up on a relationship just because it isn't perfect. Every partnership has its ups and downs, and as long as the ups outweigh the downs then it's worth persisting.

Never go to sleep on an argument.

Learn from past relationship break-ups, but don't fixate on them. Treat each new relationship as a clean slate.

To put the world in order, we must first put the nation in order; to put the nation in order, we must first put the family in order; to put the family in order, we must first cultivate our personal life; and to cultivate our personal life, we must first set our hearts right. *Confucius*

The secret of a happy marriage remains a secret – each couple has to find their own answer and their own way of being together.

Passion can bring people together, but it is never enough, on its own, to keep people together.

Almost no one is foolish enough to imagine that he automatically deserves great success in any field of activity; yet almost everyone believes that he automatically deserves success in marriage.
Sydney J. Harris

No matter how old you are, love is always young.

True love means never judging.

Everything you do determines the sort of world your children will one day live in.

Nobody can read your mind: communicate your desires effectively and regularly.

No matter what happens, every time you love someone you grow, and every time you hold back you wither.

It is better to host a good stranger than a bad brother. *African proverb*

There is not a single person alive who does not owe their very existence to the kindness of another human being.

To love someone is to allow them to be themselves.

You can never be happily married to another until you get a divorce from yourself. Successful marriage demands a certain death to self.
Jerry McCant

Love needs honesty the same way plants need sunlight.

Don't lose interest in your friends when you fall in love – invite them in to share your happiness.

It is easy to imagine that others are happier in their relationships than you are in yours. Just remember that no relationship is perfect and people are not always as happy as they seem.

Wasn't marriage, like life, unstimulating and unprofitable and somewhat empty when too well ordered and protected and guarded? Wasn't it finer, more splendid, more nourishing, when it was, like life itself, a mixture of the sordid and the magnificent; of mud and stars; of earth and flowers; of love and hate and laughter and tears and ugliness and beauty and hurt? *Edna Ferber*

Cherish your parents: they helped make you who you now are.

Love is when you feel more like yourself with another person than you do when you are on your own.

Commitment takes bravery, but it is the only way to build a love that lasts.

Love me when I least deserve it, because that is when I really need it.

Swedish proverb

Those who solve the riddle of love are the ones who ask questions of themselves rather than of others.

You should monitor your work / life balance as closely as you monitor your bank balance.

Eat and drink with your relatives; do business with strangers.

I do not think our successes can compete with those of Lourdes. There are so many more people who believe in the miracles of the Blessed Virgin than in the existence of the unconscious.
Sigmund Freud

No amount of love will bring you happiness unless you can first learn to love yourself.

Your true wealth lies in your relationships, not in your possessions.

I work with wonderful people who support me. And my beliefs are that the business needs to serve the family rather than the family serve the business. *Kathy Ireland*

Never abandon a relationship until you have tried everything you can think of to fix what is wrong with it.

Love, to be a success, must be able to overcome failures.

Only romantic love is exclusive: you can love lots of people in your life, if you love them in different ways.

Nor need we power or splendor, wide hall or lordly dome; The good, the true, the tender – these form the wealth of home. *Sarah J. Hale*

Nobody's definition of love is any more or less valid than anyone else's.

Don't try and impress others: you create the best impression when you show others your honest self.

When love develops and grows, so do you.

If you can create an honourable livelihood, where you take your skills and use them and you earn a living from it, it gives you a sense of freedom and allows you to balance your life the way you want. *Anita Roddick*

Sometimes love means giving your partner a gentle nudge.

There is always desire in love,
but not always love in desire.

Never try and imprison a loved one within the walls of jealousy.

A man can't make a place for himself in the sun if he keeps taking refuge under the family tree. *Helen Keller*

We all lose our physical beauty in time, but love cherishes an inner beauty that is constantly re-born.

Try and involve your children in your big decisions: they can often offer a refreshingly different perspective.

Love should be the main motivation driving everything you do.

There is something beautiful about all scars of whatever nature. A scar means the hurt is over, the wound is closed and healed, done with. *Harry Crews*

The depth of your relationships is more important than the number of them.

The family is one of nature's greatest works.

You have to be happy in your own skin before you can make anyone else happy.

Prioritize family time over everything else.

Making the decision to have a child is momentous. It is to decide forever to have your heart go walking outside your body. *Elizabeth Stone*

A walk with a loved one leaves you refreshed and inspired, even if the walk is only to the local shop.

Never let work stand between you and your loved ones.

Nothing about love is perfect. Love is sharing and treasuring imperfections.

I love people. I love my family, my children… but inside myself is a place where I live all alone and that's where you renew your springs that never dry up.
Pearl S. Buck

Finding a true new friend is one of life's greatest successes.

**And think not you can
Direct the course of love,
For love,
If it finds you worthy,
Directs your course.**
Khalil Gibran

Strangers are just friends you haven't met yet – make the effort to talk to at least one new person every day.

In family life, love is the oil that eases friction, the cement that binds closer together, and the music that brings harmony.
Eva Burrows

Talk to your loved ones. Even if you feel inarticulate, it is important to keep communicating as best you can.

If at least one other person truly, deeply cares about you, then you can consider yourself a success.

Becoming responsible adults is no longer a matter of whether children hang up their pajamas or put dirty towels in the hamper, but whether they care about themselves and others – and whether they see everyday chores as related to how we treat this planet. *Eda LeShan*

True love is not something that the mind can understand. Follow your heart, it knows the right answer.

Providing for your family doesn't just mean putting food on the table: it also means putting smiles on their faces.

Those that go searching for love only manifest their own lovelessness, and the loveless never find love, only the loving find love, and they never have to seek for it. *D. H. Lawrence*

Work to live, don't live to work.

Don't marry the person you think you can live with; marry only the individual you think you can't live without.
James C. Dobson

Your children can teach you a great deal about life – if you allow them to.

Don't be impatient when starting out on a new relationship: sometimes love grows slowly and quietly, like the roots of a tree.

You give your car an annual check up to keep it running smoothly – why not do the same with your relationships?

It is not flesh and blood but the heart which makes us fathers and sons.
Friedrich Schiller

Don't let family life become routine: do at least one thing slightly differently each and every day.

It is never, ever too late to fall in love.

It is not a bad thing that children should occasionally, and politely, put parents in their place. *Colette*

Love endures long after material success has faded.

The happiest moments of my life have been the few which I have passed at home in the bosom of my family. *Thomas Jefferson*

The family that laughs together stays together.

Families are the compass that guide us. They are the inspiration to reach great heights, and our comfort when we occasionally falter.
Brad Henry

A house is not a home until it is filled with love.

You cannot choose your family, so respect and celebrate the differences between you rather than allowing them to drive you apart.

Make the time to catch up with old friends – the longer you leave it the more difficult it becomes to connect with them.

Give everyone you meet the benefit of the doubt, at least once.

Good-looking individuals are treated better than homely ones in virtually every social situation, from dating to trial by jury.
Martha Beck

Respect your loved ones, even when you disagree with them.

When the fireworks of passion fade, remember that the sky is beautiful too.

Perhaps the greatest social service that can be rendered by anybody to this country and to mankind is to bring up a family.
George Bernard Shaw

Put others ahead of yourself and they will repay the favour.

List a few of the things that make you and your loved ones happy. Find ways to include those things in your daily routine.

Moderation is to be admired in many areas, but you should never be moderate in love.

Stop looking for a perfect person, and learn to treasure what is good in all the imperfect people you have already met.

The bond that links your true family is not one of blood, but of respect and joy in each other's life. Rarely do members of one family grow up under the same roof. *Richard Bach*

When love is the real deal, neither party keeps a record of the profits and losses.

Every evening, share with your partner a happy experience that occurred during the day.

Don't let the fear of losing a loved one stop you from giving everything in a relationship.

You win in love by always putting yourself second.

One of the greatest diseases is to be nobody to anybody.
Mother Teresa

A true union between two human beings strengthens both partners immeasurably.

If you dream of your success helping others rather than yourself, you are far more likely to succeed.

We waste time looking for the perfect lover, instead of creating the perfect love.
Tom Robbins

Love is the upward spiral of two people constantly bringing out the best in each other.

A society grows great when old men plant trees whose shade they know they shall never sit in. *Greek proverb*

Success
at Work

All success requires hard work, but how do we ensure our activity is focused on bringing us ever closer to our dreams?

There are two kinds of people, those who do the work and those who take the credit. Try to be in the first group; there is less competition there. *Indira Gandhi*

Take pride in your work no matter how unimportant the task in hand seems.

Change out of your work clothes as soon as you get home – it will help you to switch off and relax.

Don't feel dispirited if you cannot provide for yourself from time to time. Film director James Cameron had to depend upon the 2-for-1 McDonalds coupons his mother sent him at one time!

Find a quiet spot at your place of work, and visit that spot regularly to recharge your batteries.

The person who starts out simply with the idea of getting rich won't succeed; you must have a larger ambition. There is no mystery in business success. If you do each day's task successfully, and stay faithfully within these natural operations of commercial laws which I talk so much about, and keep your head clear, you will come out all right.
J.D. Rockefeller

Whenever possible, discuss problems that arise on a project face to face rather than flagging up an issue by sending emails or leaving voicemails.

Try and get to know something about the interests of your colleagues outside of work. Making simple bonds with others will help you all to work together more effectively.

Try not to worry about work issues outside of work: if you do not give yourself time to relax then you'll only make the problems worse.

I've never consciously striven for worldy success. But once I was aware I had it I must say that I'm terrified of losing it. *Gilbert Harding*

Your work should be important to you, but if it is the most important thing in your life then something is wrong.

When work doesn't feel enjoyable, remind yourself that you are doing something necessary to facilitate future enjoyment.

Don't look down on those who are on a lower pay-grade than you. Treat everyone you meet with respect and they will respect you in return.

We all want to do what we enjoy, but sometimes that means doing things we don't enjoy along the way.

Keep hammering away and your break will come: Harrison Ford was once a carpenter.

The trouble with the rat-race is that, even if you win, you're still a rat.
Lily Tomlin

A best-seller is the gilded tomb of a mediocre talent.
Logan Pearsall Smith

The best way to get noticed is to let the quality of your work speak for itself.

Don't waste the time it takes you to commute to work: read a book, learn a language, or acquire a new skill.

Never take work frustrations out on your loved ones.

Individual commitment to a group effort – that is what makes a team work, a company work, a society work, a civilization work.
Vince Lombardi

Giving loved ones money or presents isn't nearly as important as giving loved ones the gift of yourself.

Money can't buy happiness. Never quit a job you truly enjoy just in order to make more money.

Anyone who lives within their means suffers from a lack of imagination.
Oscar Wilde

Don't view your work colleagues as rivals but as members of the same team as you – success shared with others is all the sweeter.

Make the best of whatever situation you find yourself in: Whoopie Goldberg once worked in a mortuary painting makeup on the faces of corpses.

Don't overdo it. What is the point of being a success at 39 if you drop dead at 40?

Whenever you receive an unexpected bonus, give some of it to charity. You won't miss money that was a bonus to you anyway, and you will feel better about yourself.

The more you chase money, the harder it is to catch it.

Mike Tatum

Change your route to work now and then. Breaking routines helps you to function more effectively.

Celebrate the anniversary of your business start-up or the date you began working at your current place of employment.

He that is of the opinion money will do everything may well be suspected of doing everything for money.
Benjamin Franklin

Deliver the goods and you'll soon progress: Sean Connery started out as a milkman.

If a job's worth doing, it is worth doing well.

If you're out of work you are in good company: John Steinbeck, Quentin Tarantino, Larry King, and countless other successful people have been unemployed at some point in their lives.

Value the input of those more experienced than you.

Keep workplace distractions to a minimum. A clean work space leads to increased efficiency.

To suppose, as we all suppose, that we could be rich and not behave the way the rich behave, is like saying that we could drink all day and stay sober. *L.P. Smith*

Success is not the result of making money; making money is the result of success.
Earl Nightingale

Don't be afraid to try a radical career change if that's what you really want. Hollywood movie star Christopher Walken was once a lion tamer in a circus!

Don't involve yourself in workplace gossip: stay focused on what really matters.

Every now and then lift your eyes away from what you are doing and look at the sky. Remind yourself what your dreams are, and why you are working.

With money you can buy a house but not a home.

Chinese Proverb

Don't dig your current job? Rod Stewart once worked as a gravedigger.

The more highly you value yourself, the more valuable you will be to others.

Home is where the heart is, yes, but bring your heart to your workplace too.

Borrowed money is the most common way that smart guys go broke.
Warren Buffett

There is no elevator to success. You have to take the stairs.

Never sabotage the dreams of others in order to facilitate your own success.

Success at work, like success in life, comes from hundreds of small steps.

If you can, experiment by working at different times of the day: some people are naturally 'larks' and others are 'owls'.

The moment you dread going in to work is the moment to look for another job.

Don't criticize others for not working hard enough: lead by example.

I've never been poor, only broke. Being poor is a frame of mind. Being broke is only a temporary situation.
Mike Todd

The guy at the top isn't always the guy who is really most successful.

Speak plainly and honestly when asked your opinion. Don't try and second-guess what the other person might want to hear.

You have reached the pinnacle of success as soon as you become uninterested in money, compliments, or publicity.
Thomas Wolfe

If you feel your current job is beneath you, remind yourself that everyone had to start somewhere.

I put all my genius into my life. I put only my talent into my works.
Oscar Wilde

If the weather's nice, try walking to work. You may be surprised at how the sights and smells invigorate you.

Brad Pitt once danced in a chicken costume for a living. The only way is up!

If two brothers fight over their father's land, it is a stranger who will enjoy their sweat and labour.
African proverb

The
Spirit of
Success

Why do some people, who on the face of it seem successful, feel empty and lost in the very midst of their achievement? How do we maintain an inner equilibrium whilst striving to be even better at what we do?

A people that values its privileges above its principles soon loses both.
Dwight D. Eisenhower

A candle loses nothing by lighting another candle.

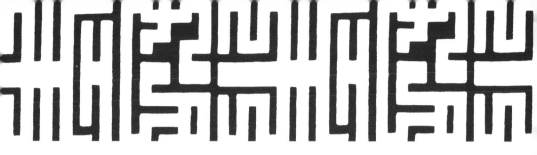

You are successful if you add more to the world than the world gives to you.

Another world is not only possible, she is on her way. On a quiet day, I can hear her breathing. *Arundhati Roy*

Instead of trying to find reasons why you can't, try and find reasons why you can.

You will only ever feel good if you do good first.

The spirit is always young, no matter how old the flesh.

Why should we live with such hurry and waste in life? We are determined to be starved before we are hungry. Men say that a stitch in time saves nine, and so they take a thousand stitches today to save nine tomorrow.

Henry David Thoreau

Whenever you feel weak, remind yourself that perseverance is more important than strength.

To be successful you must overcome your fears, not ignore them.

What is happening in the outside world is far less important than what is happening inside you.

Success need not lead to excess: you can be happy and *still* live modestly.

Until he extends his circle of compassion to include all living things, man will not himself find peace.
Albert Schweitzer

Live life one moment at a time, it is a gift to be savoured.

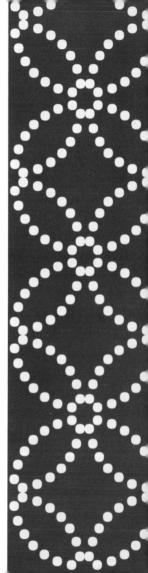

Most people are more frightened by the thought of doing something than they ever are whilst actually doing something.

Music feeds the soul: take regular meals of your favourite tunes.

It is more shameful to mistrust one's friends than to be deceived by them. *François de La Rochefoucauld*

Sometimes doing nothing can be productive – it cleanses the mind of impurities.

Every minute that you truly believe you can become successful brings that success a minute closer.

Just as it is easy to ignore the flecks of gold deposited by a stream, so it is easy to ignore small successes and see only failure.

It is no measure of health to be well adjusted to a profoundly sick society. *Jiddu Krishnamurti*

Remember to have fun: we rapidly lose interest in life when it becomes dull.

Excellence is not an accomplishment. It is a spirit, a never ending process.
Lawrence M. Miller

If you're feeling blue, take some exercise – it often helps lift the spirit.

This is the final test of a gentleman: his respect for those who can be of no possible value to him. *William Lyon Phelps*

Investigate good causes that you might help once you become successful. Sometimes helping others provides a greater motivation than helping yourself.

After you have pushed yourself hard, relax. Play is just as important as work.

Some people strengthen the society just by being the kind of people they are. *John W. Garner*

Don't just share your burdens with your friends, share good news with them too.

Just because you have to sell your labour, doesn't mean you have to sell your soul.

The only infallible rule we know is that the man who is always talking about being a gentleman never is one.
Robert Smith Surtees

How far you go in life depends on your being tender with the young, compassionate with the aged, sympathetic with the striving and tolerant of the weak and strong. Because someday in life you will have been all of these.

George Washington Carver

Before criticizing a man, walk a mile in his shoes.

Success is always a work in progress, so don't feel dispirited if you sometimes feel that you are not succeeding.

Always leave yourself time to dream: dreams are the blueprints you use to build success.

Fame is proof that the people are gullible. *Ralph Waldo Emerson*

Uneasy lies the head that wears a crown. *Shakespeare*

Good things don't come to those who wait: they come to those who invite them in.

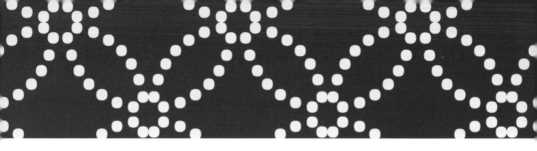

It is impossible to go through life without trust. That is to be imprisoned in the worst cell of all – oneself.
Graham Greene

What you believe is less important than *that* you believe.

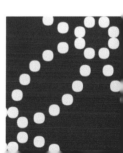

It is necessary to the happiness of man that he be mentally faithful to himself.
Thomas Paine

Visualize the goal you most want to achieve as the end point of a walk in your neighbourhood.
Then take that walk, and celebrate when you reach the finishing line.

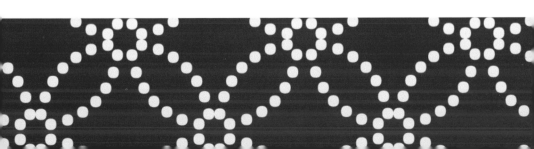

Write down something positive you have achieved today, even if it is only something small. Success rarely happens in a single moment, it comes as the result of thousands of tiny steps forwards.

Quiet minds cannot be perplexed or frightened, but go on in fortune or misfortune at their own private pace, like a clock during a thunderstorm.
Robert Louis Stevenson

It takes but one positive thought when given a chance to survive and thrive to overpower an entire army of negative thoughts. *Robert H. Schuller*

Remember your past successes and you will be half way towards recreating them.

Write thank you letters to those who have helped you: the time and effort spent will make you feel positive about yourself – which means you will have been helped all over again.

Be kind to those you meet on the way up – you may meet them again on the way down.

Make a house of cards, using one playing card to represent each of the obstacles preventing you from becoming successful. Then take a deep breath and blow the house down.

A foolish man may be known by six things: anger without cause, speech without profit, change without progress, inquiry without object, putting trust in a stranger, and mistaking foes for friends. *Arabian proverb*

Music has the power to shift our moods and calm our minds. Let a favourite track heal your wounds at the end of a difficult day.

Giving your most difficult challenge a humorous nickname can help make it seem less threatening.

It's the repetition of affirmations that leads to belief. And once that belief becomes a deep conviction, things begin to happen. *Claude M. Bristol*

Refine your dreams everyday until they shine like diamonds.

The successful tend to focus on the long run rather than the short run.

The secret of success is consistency of purpose.
Benjamin Disraeli

Do not try and change the world: it is enough to change yourself.

Take a moment at the end of every day to just relax and meditate. It will help you to put any problems into perspective, and prepare you for a good night's sleep.

Remember that no matter how poor you are, if somebody loves you, then you are rich.

If you love what you are doing, you will be successful.
Albert Schweitzer

It is better to be in chains with friends, than to be in a garden with strangers.
African proverb

The Guides

Words of advice from those who have made it – and a few words of warning from those who have not. Follow in their footsteps, or make a new path of your own: the choice is yours.

I dread success. To have succeeded is to have finished one's business on earth, like the male spider, who is killed by the female the moment he has succeeded in courtship. I like a state of continual becoming, with a goal in front and not behind.

George Bernard Shaw

There is no point at which you can say, 'Well, I'm successful now. I might as well take a nap'. *Carrie Fisher*

Everyone has talent. What is rare is the courage to follow talent to the dark place where it leads. *Erica Jong*

My mother said to me, 'If you become a soldier, you'll be a general; if you become a monk, you'll end up as the Pope'. Instead, I became a painter and wound up as Picasso.

Pablo Picasso

The worst part of success is to try to find someone who is happy for you. *Bette Midler*

'Tis not in mortals to command success, But we'll do more, Sempronius; we'll deserve it. *Joseph Addison*

Don't wait for your ship to come in, and feel angry and cheated when it doesn't. Get going with something small. *Irene Kassorla*

Being the richest man in the cemetery doesn't matter to me. Going to bed at night saying we've done something wonderful, that's what matters to me.
Steve Jobs

I figured that if I said it enough, I would convince the world that I really was the greatest. *Muhammad Ali*

Life is what we make it, always has been, always will be. *Grandma Moses*

It is very hard to be a female leader. While it is assumed that any man, no matter how tough, has a soft side… any female leader is assumed to be one-dimensional. *Billie Jean King*

Humanity I love you because you would rather black the boots of success than enquire whose soul dangles from his watch-chain. *E.E. Cummings*

Human successes, like human failures, are composed of one action at a time and achieved by one person at a time.
Patsy H. Sampson

Just don't give up trying to do what you really want to do. Where there is love and inspiration, I don't think you can go wrong. ***Ella Fitzgerald***

I think I fail a bit less than everyone else. *Jack Nicklaus*

I still have my feet on the ground, I just wear better shoes. *Oprah Winfrey*

You see things that are and say 'Why?' But I dream of things that never were and say 'Why not?' *George Bernard Shaw*

Failures are finger posts on the road to achievement. *C. S. Lewis*

I believe that a lot of our striving after the symbols and levers of success is due to a basic insecurity, a need to prove ourselves. That done, grown up at last, we are free to stop pretending. *Charles Handy*

You may be disappointed if you fail, but you are doomed if you don't try. *Beverly Sills*

Perseverance is failing nineteen times and succeeding the twentieth. *Julie Andrews*

The battles that count aren't the ones for gold medals. The struggles within yourself – the invisible, inevitable battles inside all of us – that's where it's at. *Jesse Owens*

A bird doesn't sing because it has an answer, it sings because it has a song.
Maya Angelou

Discovery consists of seeing what everyone else has seen and thinking what no one else has thought. *Albert Szent-Gyorgyi*

Discard hard and fast rules. Victory is the only thing that matters and this cannot be achieved by adhering to conventional canons. *Sun-tzu*

The greatest danger for most of us is not that our aim is too high and we miss it, but that it is too low and we reach it. *Michelangelo*

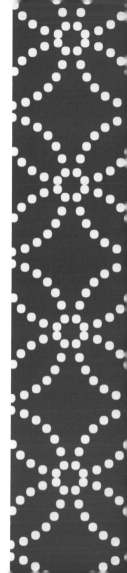

There is only one thing that makes a dream impossible to achieve: the fear of failure.
Paulo Coelho

You don't get to choose how you're going to die, or when. You can only decide how you're going to live now. *Joan Baez*

You don't pay the price for success. You enjoy the price for success. *Zig Ziglar*

Who is more deprived and alone than the man who has achieved his dream? *Brendan Francis*

I think that everything is possible as long as you put your mind to it and you put the work and time into it. I think your mind really controls everything. *Michael Phelps*

When you are aspiring to the highest place, it is honourable to reach the second or even the third rank. **Cicero**

I would sooner fail than not be among the greatest. *John Keats*

Only those who risk going too far can possibly find out how far one can go. *T. S. Eliot*

Failure? I never encountered it. All I ever met were temporary setbacks.
Dottie Walters

For all sad words of tongue and pen, the saddest are those 'It might have been'.
John Greenleaf Whittier

First say to yourself what you would be; and then do what you have to do. *Epictetus*

What counts is not necessarily the size of the dog in the fight – it's the size of the fight in the dog. *Dwight D. Eisenhower*

Men do less than they ought, unless they do all that they can. *Thomas Carlyle*

Take the first step in faith. You don't have to see the whole staircase, just take the first step.
Martin Luther King Jr.

Never let inexperience get in the way of ambition. *Terry Josephson*

Be like a postage stamp. Stick to one thing until you get there. *Josh Billings*

One of the greatest discoveries a man makes, one of his great surprises, is to find he can do what he was afraid he couldn't do. *Henry Ford*

If you go to work on your goals, your goals will go to work on you. If you go to work on your plan, your plan will go to work on you. Whatever good things we build end up building us. *Jim Rohn*

Get busy living, or get busy dying. *Stephen King*

Even if you're on the right track, you'll get run over if you just sit there. *Will Rogers*

It took us so long to realize that a purpose of human life, no matter who is controlling it, is to love whoever is around to be loved. *Kurt Vonnegut*

Use what talents you possess; the woods would be very silent if no birds sang except those that sang best.
Henry Van Dyke

Character, in great and little things, means carrying through what you feel able to do. *Goethe*

Dreams come true; without that possibility, nature would not incite us to have them. *John Updike*

As long as you're going to be thinking anyway, think big. *Donald Trump*

A goal is a dream with a deadline. *Napoleon Hill*

To achieve the impossible, it is precisely the unthinkable that must be thought.
Tom Robbins

You only live once, but if you do it right, once is enough.
Mae West

Successful and unsuccessful people do not vary greatly in their abilities. They vary in their desires to reach their potential. *John Maxwell*

Dream no small dreams, for they have no power to stir the souls of men.
Victor Hugo

I have found no greater satisfaction than achieving success through honest dealing and strict adherence to the view that, for you to gain, those you deal with should gain as well.
Alan Greenspan

Most of our obstacles would melt away if, instead of cowering before them, we should make up our minds to walk boldly through them.
Orison Swett Marden

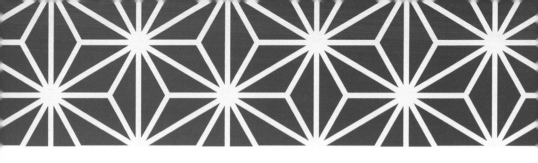

Would you like me to give you a formula for success? It's quite simple, really. Double your rate of failure. You are thinking of failure as the enemy of success. But it isn't at all. You can be discouraged by failure or you can learn from it, so go ahead and make mistakes. Make all you can. Because remember that's where you will find success. *Thomas J. Watson*

Lord, grant that I might always desire more than I can accomplish.
Michelangelo

Successful people ask better questions, and as a result, they get better answers.
Anthony Robbins

The secret of success is to do the common things uncommonly well.
John D. Rockefeller

Never give up, for that is just the place and time that the tide will turn.
Harriet Beecher Stowe

Man is born to live, not to prepare for life.
Boris Pasternak

Be patient with yourself. Self-growth is tender; it's holy ground. There's no greater investment. *Stephen Covey*

There is no such thing as can't, only won't. If you're qualified, all it takes is a burning desire to accomplish, to make a change. Go forward, go backward. Whatever it takes! But you can't blame other people or society in general. It all comes from your mind. When we do the impossible we realize we are special people.

Jan Ashford

Knowledge may give weight, but accomplishments give lustre, and many more people see than weigh.
Earl of Chesterfield

The creation of something new is not accomplished by the intellect but by the play instinct acting from inner necessity. The creative mind plays with the objects it loves.
Carl Jung

When it comes to getting things done, we need fewer architects and more bricklayers. *Colleen C. Barrett*

Don't ever forget two things I'm going to tell you. One, don't believe everything that's written about you. Two, don't pick up too many checks.
Babe Ruth

The public is a thick-skinned beast and you have to keep whacking away on its hide to let it know you're there. *Walt Whitman*

Politics is the art of the possible; creativity is the art of the impossible. *Ben Okri*

You must learn day by day, year by year, to broaden your horizon. The more things you love, the more you are interested in, the more you enjoy, the more you are indignant about, the more you have left when anything happens. *Ethel Barrymore*

Our deepest fear is not that we are inadequate. Our deepest fear is that we are powerful beyond measure. It is our light, not our darkness, that most frightens us. We ask ourselves: 'Who am I to be brilliant, gorgeous, talented and fabulous?' Actually, who are you not to be? *Nelson Mandela*

You can always become better. *Tiger Woods*

Those who want to succeed will find a way; those who don't will find an excuse. *Leo Aguila*

If children have the ability to ignore all odds and percentages, then maybe we can all learn from them. When you think about it, what other choice is there but to hope? We have two options, medically and emotionally: give up, or Fight Like Hell. *Lance Armstrong*

We are not what we know but what we are willing to learn. *Mary Catherine Bateson*

If you can dream – and not make dreams your master; If you can think – and not make thought your aim; If you can meet with triumph and disaster And treat those two impostors just the same... Yours is the Earth and everything that's in it.
Rudyard Kipling

Success is not about the background you're from, it's about the confidence you have and the effort you're willing to invest. *Michelle Obama*

Far away there in the sunshine are my highest aspirations. I may not reach them, but I can look up and see their beauty, believe in them, and try to follow where they lead. *Louisa May Alcott*

Experience is a great advantage. The problem is that when you get the experience, you're too damned old to do anything about it.
Jimmy Connors

Always bear in mind that your own resolution to succeed is more important than any other one thing.
Abraham Lincoln

The secret of getting ahead is getting started.
Sally Berger

A person always doing his or her best becomes a natural leader, just by example.
Joe DiMaggio

Don't compromise yourself. You are all you've got. *Janis Joplin*

I owe my success to having listened respectfully to the very best advice, and then going away and doing the exact opposite. *G.K. Chesterton*

When I am working on a problem I never think about beauty. I only think about how to solve the problem. But when I have finished, if the solution is not beautiful, I know it is wrong.
Buckminster Fuller

Work for something because it is good, not just because it stands a chance to succeed.
Vaclav Havel

I can honestly say that I was never affected by the question of the success of an undertaking. If I felt it was the right thing to do, I was for it regardless of the possible outcome. *Golda Meir*

A hero is someone right who doesn't change. *George Foreman*

In today's society a good many people seem to have the idea that if one is born without talent, there is nothing he can do about it; they simply resign themselves to what they consider their 'fate'. Consequently they go through life without living it to the fullest or ever knowing life's true joy. That is man's greatest tragedy.
Shinichi Suzuki

Work, alternated with needful rest, is the salvation of man or woman.

Antoinette Brown Blackwell

The big divide in this country is not between Democrats and Republicans, or women and men, but between talkers and doers. *Thomas Sowell*

I think I did pretty well, considering I started out with nothing but a bunch of blank paper. *Steve Martin*

Those who have succeeded at anything and don't mention luck are kidding themselves. *Larry King*

Time is our most valuable asset, yet we tend to waste it, kill it, and spend it rather than invest it. *Jim Rohn*

I believe in the impossible because no one else does.

Florence Griffith Joyner

A wise man should have money in his head, but not in his heart. *Jonathan Swift*

The writer who possesses the creative gift owns something of which he is not always master – something that at times strangely wills and works for itself. *Charlotte Brontë*

Your current situation is no indication of your ultimate potential. *Anthony Robbins*

All that is necessary to break the spell of inertia and frustration is this: Act as if it were impossible to fail. That is the talisman, the formula, the command of right-about-face which turns us from failure towards success. *Dorothea Brande*

First, I believe that this nation should commit itself to achieving the goal, before this decade is out, of landing a man on the moon and returning him safely to the earth. I believe we should go to the moon. But there is no sense in agreeing or desiring that the United States take an affirmative position in outer space, unless we are prepared to do the work and bear the burdens to make it successful. *John F Kennedy*

There could be no honour in a sure success, but much might be wrested from a sure defeat. *T.E. Lawrence*

Aim at heaven and you will get earth thrown in. Aim at earth and you get neither. *C. S. Lewis*

A champion is afraid of losing. Everyone else is afraid of winning.
Billie Jean King

It is our attitude at the beginning of a difficult task which, more than anything else, will affect its successful outcome.
William James

Striving for excellence motivates you; striving for perfection is demoralizing. *Harriet Braiker*

No success in public life can compensate for failure in the home.
Benjamin Disraeli

Transmission of documents via telephone wires is possible in principle, but the apparatus required is so expensive that it will never become a practical proposition. *Dennis Gabor*

With a group of bankers I always had the feeling that success was measured by the extent one gave nothing away. *Lord Longford*

A strong, positive self-image is the best possible preparation for success. *Joyce Brothers*

You can't try to do things. You simply must do things. *Ray Bradbury*

The real risk is doing nothing. *Denis Waitley*

No one would speak much in society if he were aware how often we misunderstand others. *Johann Goethe*

To see is to forget the name of the thing one sees. *Paul Valéry*

Man's reach should exceed his grasp, or what's a heaven for? *Robert Browning*

All the world's a stage and most of us are desperately unrehearsed. *Sean O'Casey*

The things we fear most in organizations – fluctuations, disturbances, imbalances – are the primary sources of creativity. *Margaret J. Wheatley*

If age imparted wisdom, there wouldn't be any old fools.
Claudia Young

The object of life is not to be on the side of the majority, but to escape finding oneself in the ranks of the insane.
Marcus Aurelius

Winning may not be everything, but losing has little to recommend it. *Dianne Feinstein*

Again, you can't connect the dots looking forward; you can only connect them looking backwards. So you have to trust that the dots will somehow connect in your future. You have to trust in something – your gut, destiny, life, karma, whatever. This approach has never let me down, and it has made all the difference in my life. *Steve Jobs*

I spent 90% of my money on women and drink. The rest I wasted. *George Best*

I believe you are your work. Don't trade the stuff of your life, time, for nothing more than dollars. That's a rotten bargain. *Rita Mae Brown*

We build too many walls and not enough bridges. *Isaac Newton*

A great social success is a pretty girl
who plays her cards as carefully as if she
were plain. *F. Scott Fitzgerald*

Some speak of the future,
My love she speaks softly,
She knows there's no success like failure
And that failure's no success at all.
Bob Dylan

If the world should blow itself up, the last audible voice would be that of an expert saying it can't be done. *Peter Ustinov*

I never see what has been done; I only see what remains to be done. *Marie Curie*

Long and Winding Road

The road to success can sometimes feel long, and everybody takes a wrong turn now and then. In this section we explore how to deal with setbacks and disappointments, so that you stay on track no matter what life throws at you.

**'Tis a lesson you should heed,
Try, try again.
If at first you don't succeed,
Try, try again.** *W.E. Hickson*

Do your research: the unknown is more terrifying than anything else, so conquer your fears by examining the potential consequences of your actions. Often you'll find that your fears melt away when you shine a light upon them.

Embrace mistakes rather than running from them. Think of your mistakes as guides telling you when to try a different path.

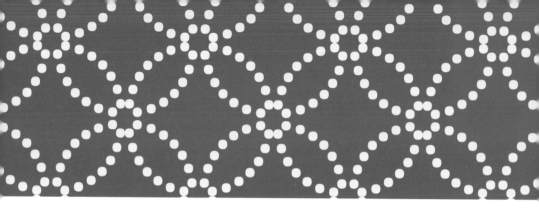

Remember that higher risks offer higher rewards. Playing safe is actually very risky, because it means you will miss out on the rewards you could have achieved if you had been prepared to really go for it.

Experience is not what happens to a man; it is what a man does with what happens to him. *Aldous Huxley*

Outsourcing advisors, KPMG surveyed 100 of the most successful companies in the world, and found that 70% of organizations had suffered at least one project failure in the previous 12 months. Which just goes to show that even the best fail sometimes…

Chasing success can be more exhilarating than actually achieving success: be careful what you wish for.

Success is counted sweetest
By those who ne'er succeed.
To comprehend a nectar
Requires sorest need.
Emily Dickinson

Most failures are due to people simply giving up before they are successful.

Plan not just how you will achieve success, but also how you will handle success.

Make sure that each mistake you make is a mistake you won't make again.

Avoiding criticism is easy – just do nothing and say nothing. But in order to achieve anything of worth, you have to learn to cope with criticism.

Keep your eye on the big picture, and don't allow yourself to be distracted by temporary setbacks.

Once you embrace unpleasant news not as a negative but as evidence of a need for change, you aren't defeated by it. You're learning from it.
Bill Gates

Don't be afraid to set yourself truly challenging goals, and don't be too disappointed if you then fail to achieve them. Challenging yourself *always* helps you grow.

Van Gogh died in poverty, but nobody remembers the wealthy art collectors who once snubbed him.

Many a champion had to get up off the canvas in order to win the fight.

You owe it to yourself to be the best you can, and the only way to pay off the debt is hard work.

Yes, he is good – so good one asks oneself why he is not better.
Ivy Compton-Burnett on Trollope

Ask yourself 'what's the worst that can happen?' The fear of failing is usually worse than the reality.

It isn't failure when you fall down; it is only failure when you don't get back up.

You don't have to be infallible to be invincible.

Every moment is a fresh start.

Integrity is so perishable in the summer months of success.
Vanessa Redgrave

The most successful basketball player in recent history, Michael Jordan, was once cut from his high-school basketball team. Keep going!

The right kind of failure can lead to a much stronger future success.

Constantly refine and improve your plans, just as a spider constantly repairs its web.

The best thing to do when you fall off a horse is to get right back in the saddle. Deal with failure in the same way.

Don't let success seduce you into thinking you cannot fail.

George Orwell's famous novel *Animal Farm* was initially rejected by the Knopf publishing house on the grounds that 'it is impossible to sell animals to raise in the U.S.' Don't allow criticism to dull your enthusiasm.

It is a mistake to suppose that men succeed through success; they much oftener succeed through failures. Precept, study, advice, and example could never have taught them so well as failure has done. *Samuel Smiles*

More haste less speed: do things properly first time around, or it will take you longer in the end.

Bill Gates started a business to analyze car traffic flow. When it flopped, he went into the computer business instead – and became the wealthiest man on the planet as a result.

Better to try and fail than never to try at all.

Ability can take you to the top, but it takes character to keep you there.

Good people are good because they've come to wisdom through failure. We get very little wisdom from success, you know.

William Saroyan

Walt Disney's first animation studio folded after just a month. He still went 'to infinity and beyond'!

Failure is the foundation of success;
if one plan doesn't work, change the plan but never the goal.

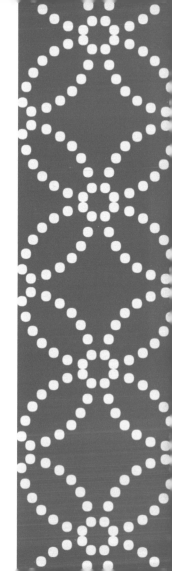

Success has many fathers, while defeat is an orphan.

A thing easy to get is easy to lose.

Success is how high you bounce when you hit bottom.

It was a sad day when the Truman & Jacobson haberdashery store in Kansas City closed down in 1922. But one of the owners knew how to handle setbacks: Harry Truman went on to become president of the United States.

An orderly retreat has led to ultimate victory in many of history's key battles.

When the roof falls in, rejoice in the beauty of the clouds.

The most successful people are those who are good at plan B.
James Yorke

There is no pause button on life or on success – so play!

Do it your way, not the way others say it should be done.

Remember The Charge Of The Light Brigade: no-one doubts the bravery of those who took part, but it is still considered a military disaster. Take risks, yes, but don't be reckless.

You always pass failure on your way to success.

Mickey Rooney

Whenever you find the key to success, someone changes the lock.

Truly great people never make others feel small, but instead make others feel that they too can become successful.

J.K. Rowling's best-selling *Harry Potter* books were rejected by 12 publishers before making it into print.

Thankfully, persistence is a great substitute for talent.
Steve Martin

Success is not final, failure is not fatal: it is the courage to continue that counts. *Winston Churchill*

Failure doesn't dilute success, it distills it.

At the end of each day, whether it has been a good day or a bad day, pledge to do better tomorrow.

There are many paths to the top of the mountain, but the view is just as good no matter which of the paths you take.

Woody Allen was thrown out of film school before he went on to become an Oscar winning writer and director.

There are some defeats more triumphant than victories.

Michel de Montaigne

What we do repeatedly is what we become. Therefore, make sure you do the small things brilliantly, as you will be doing small things every day of your life.

The most valuable lessons
are the ones you learn after
you think you know it all.

Nothing travels faster
than the speed of
light with the possible
exception of bad
news, which obeys its
own special laws.
Douglas Adams

The
Successful
Smile

What is the point of succeeding if you can't enjoy your success? This is a collection of witty sayings about the fluctuating fortunes of those who have been brave enough to go in pursuit of their dreams.

Both optimists and pessimists contribute to our society. The optimist invents the airplane and the pessimist the parachute. *G.B. Stern*

He was a self-made man who owed his lack of success to nobody. *Joseph Heller*

I've got to keep breathing. It'll be my worst business mistake if I don't.
Steve Martin

Better to remain silent and be thought a fool, than to open your mouth and remove all doubt.

Important families are like potatoes. The best parts are underground.
Francis Bacon

Some cause happiness wherever they go; others whenever they go.
Oscar Wilde

The darkest hour of any man's life is when he sits down to plan how to get money without earning it. *Horace Greeley*

Human beings, who are almost unique in having the ability to learn from the experience of others, are also remarkable for their apparent disinclination to do so. *Douglas Adams*

Having children makes you no more a parent than having a piano makes you a pianist. *Michael Levine*

He had a genius for backing into the limelight.
Lowell Thomas on T.E. Lawrence

It is the ordinary woman who knows something about love. The gorgeous ones are too busy being gorgeous.

Katharine Hepburn

When a person with money meets a person with experience, the person with the experience winds up with the money and the person with the money winds up with the experience. *Harvey MacKay*

Every morning I get up and look through the Forbes list of the richest people in America. If I'm not there, I go to work. *Robert Orben*

Any fool can criticize,
and many of them do.
Archbishop C. Garbett

**More marriages might survive if the partners
realized that sometimes the better comes
after the worse.** *Doug Larson*

Govern a family as you would cook a small fish – very gently. *Chinese proverb*

I made my money the old fashioned way. I was very nice to a wealthy relative right before he died. *Malcolm Forbes*

Many a man owes his success to his first wife and his second wife to his success. *Jim Backus*

Money, it turned out, was exactly like sex, you thought of nothing else if you didn't have it and thought of other things if you did. *James Baldwin*

The best husbands are healthy and absent. *Japanese proverb*

There is scarcely an instance of a man who has made a fortune by speculation, and kept it. *Andrew Carnegie*

To be clever enough to get all the money, one must be stupid enough to want it.
G.K. Chesterton

Civilization is unbearable, but it is less unbearable at the top.
Timothy Leary

A critic is a man who knows the way but can't drive the car. *Kenneth Tynan*

Money couldn't buy friends, but you get a better class of enemy. *Spike Milligan*

If you haven't time to respond to a tug at your pants leg, your schedule is too crowded. *Robert Brault*

The reason grandparents and grandchildren get along so well is that they have a common enemy.
Sam Levenson

Success is something that always comes faster to the person your partner almost married.

I won't say ours was a tough school, but we had our own coroner. We used to write essays like 'what I'm going to be if I grow up'. *Lenny Bruce*

While we try to teach our children all about life, Our children teach us what life is all about.
Angela Schwindt

I may not have gone where I intended to go, but I think I have ended up where I intended to be.
Douglas Adams

It's kind of fun to do the impossible.
Walt Disney

Like all the best families, we have our share of eccentricities, of impetuous and wayward youngsters and of family disagreements. *Queen Elizabeth II*

To love oneself is the beginning of a lifelong romance.
Oscar Wilde

When I think of all the crap I learned in high school, it's a wonder I can think at all. *Paul Simon*

It is better to fail in originality than to succeed in imitation. *Herman Melville*

There was never a child so lovely but his mother was glad to get him to sleep.
Ralph Waldo Emerson

Pray that success will not come any faster than you are able to endure it.
Elbert Hubbard

Behind every successful man, there is a surprised woman.

The closer one gets to the top, the more one finds there is no 'top'.
Nancy Barcus

Success seems to be largely a matter of hanging on after others have let go.
William Feather

If at first you don't succeed, skydiving is not for you.
Arthur McAuliff

If you want to make an apple pie from scratch, you must first create the universe.
Carl Sagan

Victory goes to the player who makes the next-to-last mistake.
Savielly Tartakower

Two and two continue to make four, in spite of the whine of the amateur for three, or the cry of the critic for five. *James McNeill Whistler*

I have not failed. I've just found 10,000 ways that won't work. *Thomas Edison*

In judging others, folks will work overtime for no pay. *Charles Edwin Carruthers*

Success gets easier as you get older. Once they used to expect me to come on stage, smoke a cigar, and tell jokes. Now if I just get to the stage I get a round of applause. *George Burns*

Old age is like everything else. To make a success of it, you've got to start young. *Fred Astaire*

Life is a tragedy when seen in close-up, but a comedy in long-shot.
Charlie Chaplin

The search for someone to blame is always successful.
Robert Half

A man's got to take a lot of punishment to write a really funny book. *Ernest Hemingway*

If at first you don't succeed, try, try again. Then give up. There's no use in being a damn fool about it. *W.C. Fields*

Age is strictly a case of mind over matter. If you don't mind, it doesn't matter.
Jack Benny

It's too bad I'm not as wonderful a person as they say I am, because the world could use a few people like that. *Alan Alda*

Each success only buys an admission ticket to a more difficult problem. *Henry Kissinger*

For an actress to be a success, she must have the face of a Venus, the brains of a Minerva, the grace of Terpsichore, the memory of a MaCaulay, the figure of Juno, and the hide of a rhinoceros.

Ethel Barrymore

If you can count your money, then you're not a rich man.

John Paul Getty

If everything seems under control, you're just not going fast enough. *Mario Andretti*

You live and learn. At any rate, you live. *Douglas Adams*